Sam's Birthday

by Judy Nayer
illustrated by Sally Vitsky

Scott Foresman

Editorial Offices: Glenview, Illinois • New York, New York
Sales Offices: Reading, Massachusetts • Duluth, Georgia
Glenview, Illinois • Carrollton, Texas • Menlo Park, California

Sam Dinosaur was walking to school. He saw Rex.

"Hello, Rex!" said Sam. "Today is my birthday! Will you play with me after school?"

"Sorry, Sam," said Rex.
"I'm busy today."

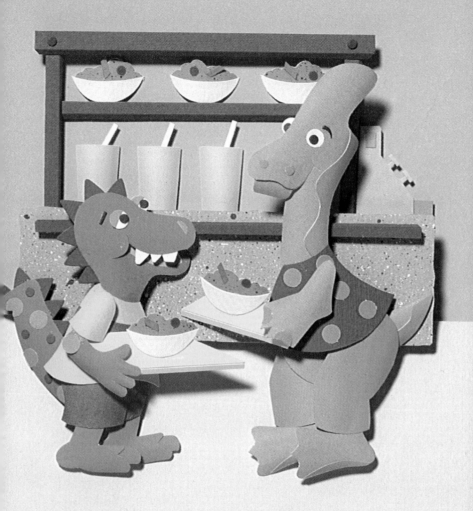

Next, Sam saw Dan. "Hello, Dan!" he said. "Today is my birthday! Will you play with me after school?"

"Sorry, Sam," said Dan.
"I'm busy today."

Next, Sam saw Pat. "Hello,
Pat!" he said. "Today is my
birthday! Will you play with me
after school?"

"Sorry, Sam," said Pat.
"I'm busy today."
One after another, in order, all of
Sam's friends said the same thing.

Sam was sad!

Sam was very sad!

Then the bell rang.
"Surprise!" said the dinosaurs.

"I thought you were busy,"
said Sam.

"We were busy!" said Rex. "I was busy buying you a present!"

"I was busy making you a card!" said Dan.

"I was busy baking you a cake!" said Pat.

"We were busy planning your
party!" said the dinosaurs.
"Happy Birthday, Sam!"